39

The Education demanded by the People of the U. States.

A

DISCOURSE

DELIVERED AT

UNION COLLEGE, SCHENECTADY,

JULY 25, 1854,

ON THE OCCASION OF

THE FIFTIETH ANNIVERSARY OF THE PRESIDENCY OF

ELIPHALET NOTT, D. D., LL. D.

BY

FRANCIS WAYLAND,

PRESIDENT OF BROWN UNIVERSITY.

BOSTON:
PHILLIPS, SAMPSON, AND COMPANY.
1855.

WRIGHT AND HASTY, PRINTERS, 3 WATER STREET, BOSTON.

DISCOURSE.

GENTLEMEN, ALUMNI OF UNION COLLEGE:

THE reason of my appearing before you may be very briefly told. The man, whom every Graduate of Union College loves as a friend and venerates as a parent, thought proper to request me to perform this service. Though gray hairs have long since admonished me to decline all similar engagements, yet an intimation from him, to whom I owe more than to any other living man, was as imperative as when, in yonder halls, a thoughtless boy, I first listened to those counsels in which wisdom and eloquence were so marvelously blended. I am as well aware as any of you can be, of my inability to meet the just demands of this occasion. Gladly, therefore, would I have learned that the choice of my honored instructor had fallen upon some more gifted pupil. But, in the words of Dr. Johnson, on a different occasion, "It was not for me to bandy compliments with my sovereign. The king said it, and it was so." Bowing to an authority which it would be treason to call in question, you behold me, therefore, already at my work.

I am requested to discuss the principles which should govern the system of collegiate education in our age and country.

Let us in the first place consider some of the principles which should govern education in general.

By education we mean that culture either of body or mind, which shall enable us the better to discharge the duties of our present probation and prepare for the results which shall emerge from that probation hereafter. It comprehends, therefore, every interest of humanity. Its influence must be felt throughout the ages of an endless duration. Necessity, obliges us, however, on this occasion, to treat only of the culture of our intellectual nature.

If you will allow me to commence with an elementary thought, I would remark, that every act of the mind *ends* in a knowledge, sometimes only subjective, but generally both subjective and objective. Thus I am conscious of a simple emotion; here is a mental act, a mere subjective knowledge. I perceive a tree; here is a subjective consciousness and an objective knowledge. And, on the other hand, every knowledge *presupposes* an act of mind; for were there no mind, or were the mind incapable of action, knowledge would be impossible.

From this simple and obvious fact, it has naturally come to pass that men have looked upon the subject of education from two distinct points of view, as they have contemplated either the act of mind, or the knowledge in which it results. Hence, some have considered education to consist merely in the communication of knowledge; others almost entirely in the discipline of mind. If the first be our object, it will be successfully accomplished precisely in proportion to the amount and the value of the knowledge which we communicate. If, on the other hand, we desire simply to cultivate the intellect, our success must be measured by the number of faculties which we improve, and the degree of culture which we have imparted to them.

It is, I presume, for this reason, that a division has, to a considerable degree, been established between the studies which enter into our course of higher education. Some of them, of which the results are acknowledged to be in general valueless, are prosecuted on account of the mental discipline which they are supposed to impart. That they tend to nothing practical, has sometimes been deemed their appropriate excellence. Hence, some learned men have exulted rather facetiously in the "glorious inutility" of the studies which they recommend. On the other hand; there are many studies which communicate knowledge, admitted by all men to be indispensable, which are supposed to convey no mental discipline, or, at least, only that which is of the most elementary character. Hence, you at once perceive that a wide ground for debate is afforded, which writers on education have not been backward to occupy. Hence, also the various discussions on the best methods of education, which seem to me to approach with but slow and unequal steps to any definite conclusion, The studies which are most relied on for mental discipline, for instance, are the classics and the mathematics. While the advocates for these discard, almost contemptuously, all other methods of culture, they are by no means agreed among themselves. The mathematicians look with small favor upon the lovers of lexicons, and paradigms, and accents; and claim that nothing but exact science can invigorate the power of ratiocination, on which all certainty of knowledge depends. The philologists, on the other hand, inveigh in no measured terms against the narrow range of mathematical culture, and boldly affirm that it unfits men for all reasoning concerning matter actually existing, while it withers up every delicate sentiment and turns into an arid waste the entire field of our emotional nature. Here issue is joined, and I am compelled in truth to add, *adhuc sub judice lis est.*

But is it not possible to escape from the smoke and din of this controversy, and look upon this question from a somewhat higher point of view? It may, I think, be safely taken for granted, that the system of which we form a part, is the work of a Being of infinite wisdom and infinite benevolence. He made the world without us and the world within us, and he manifestly made each of them for the other. He has made knowledge, intellectual culture and progress, all equally necessary to our individual and social well-being. He abhors all castes, and desires that every one of his children shall enjoy to the full all the means of happiness which have been committed to his trust. Is it then to be supposed that he has made for our brief probation two kinds of knowledge; one necessary for the attainment of our means of happiness, but incapable of nourishing and strengthening the soul; and the other, tending to self-culture, but leading to no single practica advantage? Shall we believe that the God and Father of al has made the many to labor by blind rules for the good of the few, without the possibility of spiritual elevation; and the few to learn nothing that shall promote the happiness of the whole, living on the labors of others, selfishly building themselves up in intellectual superiority? Is it not rather to be believed, that he has made each of these ends to harmonize with the other, so that all intellectual culture shall issue in knowledge which shall confer benefits on the whole; and all knowledge properly acquired, shall in an equal degree tend to intellectual development? Did God manifest himself in the flesh, in the form of a carpenter's son, to create an intellectual aristocracy, and consign the remaining millions of our race to daily toil, excluded from every opportunity for spiritual improvement? Did he not rather appear to scatter blessings broad-cast upon all born of woman, so that every individual of the race whose form he had assumed, might cultivate to its highest perfection his intellectual and moral nature, and thus grow up into the stature of a perfect man in Christ Jesus?

These expectations seem to me to be reasonable. If so, we might surely anticipate that all knowledge acquired according to the established laws of mind, would be productive of self-culture. Nay, we might suppose that that which God had made most necessary to our existence, would be, in the highest degree, self-disciplinary. Thus every one, whatever his position, may well be supposed to possess the means of developing his own powers, and arriving at the standing of an intellectual man. There is nothing in the nature of any occupation that renders such an expectation extravagant. The uncles of Hugh Miller were highly cultivated men, reading the best books, concerning one of whom he remarks, "there are professors of natural history who know less of living nature than was known by uncle Sandy;" and yet one of them was a harness-maker, and the other a stone-mason; each laboring industriously at his calling, for daily bread, for six days in the week.

But if we take no account of the acquisition of knowledge and confine ourselves simply to intellectual culture, I apprehend that we shall arrive at substantially the same result. Suppose that our sole object is to develop the powers of the human mind. We must then first ask what are these powers. It will be sufficient for our present purpose to consider the following, as they are allowed to be the most important: Perception, by which we arrive at a knowledge of the phenomena of the world without us; Consciousness, by which we become aware of the changes in the world within us; Abstraction and Generalization, by which our knowledge of individuals becomes the knowledge of classes; Reasoning, by which we use the known to discover the unknown; Imagination, by which we construct pictures in poetry and ideals in philosophy; and Memory, by which all these various forms of past knowledge are recalled and made available for the present. I am not, however, strenuous concerning this division of the faculties of the human mind. Let him who disapproves of it, make a better for himself. I will have no controversy with him; only let him present the faculties by which the most important acts of the mind are performed, and let his description be definite, so that we may clearly understand his terminology.

Now, if such be the powers conferred on us by our Creator, it must, I think, be admitted that each of them is designed for a particular purpose, and that a human mind would be fatally deficient were any one of them wanting. In our cultivation of mind, then, we must have respect not to one or two of them, but to all; since that is the most perfect mind in which all of them are the most fully developed.

If, then, we desire to improve the intellect of man by study, it is obvious that that study will be the best adapted to our purpose which cultivates not one, but all, of these faculties, and and cultivates them all most thoroughly. We cultivate our powers of every kind by exercise, and that study will most effectually aid us in the work of self-development, which requires the original exercise of the greatest number of them.

Supposing this to be admitted, which I think will not be denied, the question will arise what studies are best adapted to our purpose. This is a question which cannot be settled by authority. We are just as capable of deciding it as the men who have gone before us. They were once like ourselves, men of the present, and their wisdom has not certainly received any addition from the slumber of centuries. They may have been able to judge correctly for the time that then *was*, but could they revisit us now, they might certainly be no better able than ourselves to judge correctly for the time that *now is*. If any of us should be heard of two hundred years hence, it would surely be strange folly for the men of A. D. 2054 to receive our sayings as oracles concerning the conditions of society which will be then existing. God gives to every age the means for perceiving its own wants and discovering the best manner of supplying them; and it is, therefore, certainly best that every age should decide such questions for itself. We cannot, certainly, decide them by authority.

There are two methods by which we can determine the truth in this matter. First, we may examine any particular study and observe the faculties of mind which it does and which it does not call into action. Every reasonable man, at all acquainted with the nature of his own mind, will be able to do this. Take, for instance, the studies which are pursued for the sake merely of discipline. Do they call into exercise one or many of our faculties? Suppose they cultivate the reasoning power, and the power of poetic combination? Do they do any thing else? If not, what have we by which to improve the powers of observation, of consciousness, of generalization, and combination, these most important and most valuable of our faculties? If, then, their range be so limited, it may be deserving of inquiry whether some studies which can improve a larger number of our faculties might not sometimes take their places; and yet more, whether they should occupy so large a portion of the time dovoted to education.

But we may examine the subject by another test. We may ask what are the results actually produced by devotion to those studies which are allowed to be merely disciplinary. We teach the mathematics to cultivate the reasoning power, and the languages to improve the imagination and the taste. We then may very properly inquire, are mathematicians better reasoners than other men, in matter not mathematical? As a student advances in the mathematics, do we find his powers of ratiocination, in any thing but the relations of quantity, to be visibly improved? Are philologists or classical students more likely to become poets, or artists, than other men, or, does their style by this mode of discipline approach more nearly to the classical models of their own, or of any other language?

It is by such considerations as these that this question is to be answered. We have long since abjured all belief in magical influences. If we cannot discover any law of nature by which a cause produces its effect, and are unable to perceive that the effect is produced, we begin to doubt whether any causation exists in the matter.

If there be any truth in the foregoing remarks, they would seem to lead us to the following conclusions:

First, that every branch of study should be so taught as to accomplish both the results of which we have been speaking; that is, that it should not only increase our knowledge, but also confer valuable discipline; and that it should not only confer valuable discipline, but also increase our knowledge; and that, if it does not accomplish both of these results, there is either some defect in our mode of teaching, or the study is imperfectly adapted to the purposes of education.

Secondly, that there seems no good reason for claiming pre-eminence for one study over another, at least in the manner to which we have been accustomed. The studies merely disciplinary have valuable practical uses. To many pursuits they are important, and to some indispensable. Let them, then, take their proper place in any system of good learning, and claim nothing more than to be judged of by their results. Let them not be the unmeaning shibboleth of a caste; but, standing on the same level with all other intellectual pursuits, be

2

valued exactly in proportion to their ability to increase the power and range and skill of the human mind, and to furnish it with that knowledge which shall most signally promote the well-being and happiness of humanity.

And, thirdly, it would seem that our whole system of instruction requires an honest, thorough and candid revision. It has been for centuries the child of authority and precedent. If those before us made it what it is, by applying to it the resources of earnest and fearless thought, I can see no reason why we, by pursuing the same course, might not improve it. God intended us for progress, and we counteract his design when we deify antiquity, and bow down and worship an opinion, not because it is either wise or true, but merely because it is ancient.

But, supposing all these questions to be settled, and that we perfectly understood the nature of the human mind, the studies best adapted to improve it, and the manner of teaching them so as best to accomplish our purpose, it might be supposed that the work of providing a system of education for a people would be easy. Such would be the case, provided that men were made in all respects precisely alike, and were placed in exactly the same circumstances. If, for instance, all men were created not only with the same faculties, but with all in precisely the same proportion; if they were all moved by the same impulses and chose the same pursuits; if they were under the same conditions of wealth, civilization and general culture, and moreover being incapable of progress, continued age after age unchanged and unchangeable, we might then easily devise a system of instruction which would never stand in need either of cultivation or improvement, but which, once established, would remain established forever.

But, the reverse of all this is the truth. Though endowed with the same faculties, we perceive that these faculties are bestowed in different degrees and in unequal proportions. In one the faculty of observation predominates; in another the subjective faculty. In one the reasoning power is vigorous; in another the power of combination. One is more capable of action; another of contemplation. In harmony with this difference of endowment, we find the choice of pursuits among men extremely dissimilar. This difference is necessary to the progress, nay, almost to the existence, of society. "If the whole body were an eye, where where the hearing. If the whole were hearing, where were the smelling." Hence we find men every where addicting themselves to different departments of labor, and this bias frequently manifests itself in early youth. One displays a taste for science, another for practice; one chooses this branch of learning, and another that; one turns instinctively to the closet, another to the forum; one to the counting-room of the merchant, and another to the shop of the mechanic; and we generally find that wherever a distinct love for any pursuit exists, it is accompanied by those mental endowments which ultimately lead to success.

But the external circumstances of men are dissimilar. In some circumstances wealth is much more universally diffused than in others, and hence the facilities for education are unlike. Government also exerts an acknowledged power in moulding the intellectual and social character of a people. The institutions of Turkey and those of Great Britain must create vast differences in the mental habitudes of the people. The amount of general knowledge which underlies the whole system of higher education, must greatly modify the form and proportions of the social edifice which we propose to erect upon it. Suppose a system of education had been devised for a nation before the invention of printing, how unsuitable would it prove for the people of this country at the present moment. It is, then, apparent, that in order to construct a system of education for any age or nation, the intellectual and social condition of that people must ever be kept in view.

And it will at once appear that this remark applies with increased force, the higher we rise in our scale of instruction.

The elementary branches of education must be the same for all. Ability to read is required by the emperor and the serf, and both must begin by learning the alphabet, and both must learn it in the same manner. Both, in order to arrive at the dignity of manhood, need to be taught to communicate their thoughts to others by writing, and both must begin with straight marks and pot-hooks. Both must be instructed in arithmetic, geography, and the correct use of their native language, and the teaching which is best for the one is best also for the other. In all this range of education, therefore, the ground is common for all.

When, however, we proceed to the more advanced branches of education, the whole scene changes. The various departments of science present themselves before us, too numerous by far, and too difficult of acquisition to be all embraced within the range of the education of any individual. A choice then becomes necessary, and this choice must be determined by the peculiar talent and bias of the pupil, the profession in life to which those views incline him, and for which they give him peculiar facilities. These will also be varied by the social condition of a people, the amount of common education generally possessed, and the character of the government for which the higher education is designed. No system of education can suit the wants of a people which does not take distinctly into view all these elementary considerations.

In speaking, then, of the system of collegiate instruction, or, that course of education which intervenes between a common school and the entrance upon the various occupations of life, we must first inquire what peculiarity may be observed in the condition of the people of the United States, which should guide our judgments in this respect.

In speaking upon this subject, I remark, in the first place, that the physical condition of the United States is, so far as I know, unparalleled in the history of man.

The facilities which we enjoy for the universal acquisition

of competence, nay, of wealth, are such as never before existed. Within the limits of the United States, stretching from the great Lakes to the Gulf of Mexico, and from the Atlantic to the Pacific, there are millions of acres of as good land as the sun shines upon, which may be had almost for the asking. The government price of this land per acre, is about half a day's wages of a journeyman mechanic. Much of it is of inexhaustible fertility, covered, far beneath the reach of the plough, with the vegetable mould of centuries. It extends through the choicest portion of the temperate zone, and occupies every variety of situation. Hence it is adapted to all the staple productions demanded either for the food or the clothing of man. Flax, hemp, cotton, and silk, here find soils and climate adapted to their most successful cultivation. Grains of every kind grow in abundance which might almost seem fabulous. Animal food fattens on the prairies and in the forest, without expense to the owner, and almost without his care.

The mineral wealth of these regions is equally remarkable. Setting aside what are called the precious metals, which, by the way, I consider of very small value, we have here as rich mines of lead, copper and iron, as can be found on the face of the earth. Add to this the eastern portion of our western domain, is one inexhaustible coal basin, containing a richer supply of fuel than is contained in all the coal fields of the world beside.

But the bounty of nature has not been exhausted by these munificent gifts. This whole region is amply supplied with rivers. The invention of the steam engine has made these rivers navigable in every direction. A boat may ply from the Falls of St. Anthony to the Gulf of Mexico, and from the borders of Pennsylvania to the regions where the buffalo and the prairie dog hold almost undisputed possession. This coal region is specially intersected with navigable rivers. Hence our western states must be ere long the manufacturers for the world. Manufactories always move towards the coal measures, and the vicinity of iron mines. The branches of these mighty rivers will bring to them the raw material from the whole of that vast valley which stretches away between the Allegany and the Rocky Mountains, and will either return the finished product to the place of its growth, or bear it to the seaboard, to supply with the means of comfort and convenience the millions of Europe.

But this is not all. The railroad has already penetrated all these regions, and is covering the west with a net-work of iron. A year or two since, and no one but the hunter, or the prospector for lead, had ever visited the Falls of St. Anthony. A few weeks ago, fifteen hundred persons, men, women and remarkable children, made an excursion to this romantic locality, hearing at every step of their progress the throb of the steam chamber, or the whistle of the locomotive. Every product of this region is thus brought at once to the most profitable market, and bears a price which compares with the price in cities.

Of the enormous increase of wealth which has thus covered this country, we can form no adequate conception. Imagination itself is staggered when the simple elements are placed before it. Let me offer a single illustration. When I was a student in this institution, and for some years afterwards, all the wheat arriving at Albany from the west, was transported on sleighs. I have seen them pass through this city in companies half a mile in length. The cost of transportation was so great, that, in the neighborhood of Geneva, the regular price of wheat was thirty-seven and a half cents a bushel. Farther west than this, the cost of carriage reduced the price so low that it could not be raised with profit. The price of land, of course, corresponded with that of its staple production. Cleveland and Chicago were then unknown, and the land on which they are built might have been purchased by the year's wages of a respectable mechanic. West of Buffalo, the whole earth was almost a *terra incognita.*

A few years afterwards, the Erie Canal, that wonderful monument to the genius, patriotism and statesmanship of De Witt Clinton, a name which I never pronounce without the profoundest emotions of veneration and gratitude, was opened. The next year wheat rose to sixty-two and a half cents per bushel. The following year it reached one dollar. From that time it has never receded, and there have been times when even that price has been doubled. The value of land, of course, rose in proportion.

The effect thus produced on this single State by the Erie Canal, has been produced throughout our whole western country by the steamer and the locomotive. They bring the markets of the world to every man's door, and, by reducing the price of transportation, place the largest share of profit in the hands of the immediate producer. Rapidity of transportation renders even the most perishable article every where marketable. The prairie chickens of Illinois and Indiana are regularly for sale in the markets of Boston and New York, and the cod and salmon of the Atlantic coast, smoke upon the tables of Cincinnati, Chicago and Indianapolis.

Now, take as the element of your calculation, the change which I have spoken of in this State, and generalizing the idea, spread this effect over the immense regions of the west, and I ask, is it possible to estimate the increase of the wealth of the United States within the period of the last thirty years? Observe the cities that have become the marts of trade for this vast region. Their annual increase in wealth surpasses belief. Observe the thousands of miles of railroad spreading in every direction, which are unable, as it would seem, to absorb our floating capital. Turn to the manufacturing cities and towns which are multiplying themselves by their own profits, on every river, and in the vicinity of every coal mine; and when you have added all this together, you will have formed but a most imperfect idea of the progress in wealth of this nation.

It requires but a moment to show that all these changes

tend to enrich not one class, but all classes. Universal and cheap means of transportation increase, as we have seen, the wealth of the producer. But they, at the same time, reduce the price of the product. As a day's labor will purchase a larger amount of flour, or clothing, or animal food, the wages of the laborer are by just so much advanced. The immense emigration to the west, reduces the number of laborers at the east, and thus, the supply falling below the demand in all the older States, the price of labor is greatly augmented. Thus the laborer receives higher wages, and his wages are worth more than before. The immensely increasing reciprocal demand for the products of the east and the west, and the vast amount of exchanges by which this demand is supplied, render it possible for merchants and manufacturers to pay higher wages than before, and yet leave for themselves a profit that accumulates around them the wealth of princes.

But another element here deserves a remark. Skill in invention, united to the miraculous power of steam, is removing from human sinews the most laborious parts of every operation. Our forging and planing, our spinning and weaving, our mowing and reaping, and threshing, our transportation, both of men and of produce, is now all done by machinery, and generally driven by steam. In my youth, I have seen the labors of the hand-loom, and observed how a strong man toiled through a very long day at his slowly increasing work. A week since, I was passing through a cotton mill, and observed a young girl of ten or twelve years of age, attending upon five looms, and while doing what was formerly the work of ten men, she walked to and fro with an air of easy independence, which a lady at a reception might be well pleased to emulate.

The result of all this it is very easy to perceive. God is thus lifting off from us that oppressive severity of toil which paralyzes intellect and benumbs the power of emotion. The mind is thus rendered physically capable of thought and reflection. The rise in the rate of wages, the greater value of wages, and the diminished number of hours of daily labor, are placing our whole population in a condition for improvement such as no country has ever before enjoyed. We see here a tendency to realize the beneficent designs of the Creator. It is evident that God intended all men to think, and to enjoy all the advantages of intellectual culture, for he has given to all men all the powers adapted to thought and culture. It is equally evident that he intended all men to labor, for labor is essential to physical health and enjoyment. And, moreover, men think the better for working, and they work the better for thinking. He, however, never intended that labor should crush the power of thought. His design concerning us will not be accomplished, until every man shall be able to secure a competence by an amount of labor which shall leave his spiritual nature free and unembarrassed, nay, the better prepared for its work on account of the physical labor in which it has been engaged.

The condition of this country looks towards the realization of this idea. In no country on earth has physical labor ever been so well remunerated. In no country has there ever been so universal an ability to acquire knowledge for ourselves, and bestow education on our children. Unless we are cursed with wicked counsels and inflamed with an insane love of conquest; unless the public conscience is debauched by oppression and injustice, which corrupts at the core all generous public spirit; unless while we persuade ourselves that we are masters, we are degraded into slaves, we may hope to see in this country a population of which no philanthropist or statesman has ever formed a conception.

I have spoken of our facilities of intercommunication. The effect of this element of our condition is deserving of a remark. We all speak the same language. We all are under the same government. There is not a man among us to whom every act of this government is not a matter of interest. But more than this: there is no part whatever of our country which is not connected by a thousand ties with every other part. A man can travel in no direction over any State of the Union, without finding some of his former neighbors, to whom nothing is more grateful than information from the ancient homestead. The present facilities of intercourse cherish this interest, and keep it ever on the alert. The amount of personal communication between the various parts of our country is absolutely incalculable, especially between the east and the west, and particularly in the Free States. This facility of intercourse is immeasurably quickened by the lines of telegraph wire stretching in every direction, uniting every portion with every other, and with every part of the civilized world.

The Atlantic steamer has not reached her berth, before the news which she brings is proclaimed in the streets of Cincinnati and St. Louis. The official signature is not dry upon a legislative act in any one of our States, before its provisions are proclaimed from the shores of the Atlantic to the banks of the Missouri. A change in the price of any staple production concerns every man in the community, and every man is anxious to satisfy himself on the subject. Thus the public mind is ever wakeful. Every man is continually forming judgments, true or false, but yet judgments, not only concerning the events in his own town or village, but events that are occurring throughout the Republic and the world. The effect of all this in diffusing a love of information, quickening mental energy, enlarging the breadth of generalization, and cultivating the love of progress, is too obvious to need illustration. The physical conditions of our country thus present as glorious a field in which to scatter broadcast the seeds of all knowledge, as the imagination of the philanthropic statesman ever conceived.

Let us next inquire what is the educational character of our people.

The Puritan ancestors of this country were men of whom the world was not worthy. England was sifted to furnish the seed with which these Northern States were planted. They left their homes, and became the inhabitants of a wilderness, in obedience to moral principle. They sought for freedom to worship God. They established a civil society on the foundation of equal rights. They well knew that equal rights could only be secured on the basis of intelligence and virtue. Here, then, they laid the corner stone of their social edifice. They determined that every citizen should be instructed in good learning, and be provided with the means of religious instruction. They were well persuaded that a people nurtured under such auspices could never be either slaves or oppressors; for he who is intelligent and just, must love liberty, as well for his neighbor as for himself. Their first care was, therefore, the establishment of schools for the whole community.

As population multiplied and wealth increased, their system of education expanded and improved. The schools have, in most of the States, been placed under legislative supervision. Private as well as public munificence, has added to their means of efficiency. Normal schools are scattering able and well instructed teachers throughout the land. Schools are liberally sustained by taxes imposed by the people on themselves. School districts are uniting to furnish themselves with instruction in the more advanced branches of learning. There is no subject which calls forth a livelier interest, in any town in New England, than the advancement of knowledge. It banishes even political hostility, and men of all parties unite with each other in carrying forward a cause, on the success of which all that we hold valuable so essentially depends. In this good work, Massachusetts, by confession, takes the lead. Within a few years she has added to her ancient glory, by passing an act authorizing every town to tax itself for the maintenance of a library; thus establishing the principle, that it is the duty of society not only to care for the instruction of the individual, but also to provide the means for rendering this instruction in the highest degree valuable.

The example of Massachusetts was early emulated by the States in her neighborhood, and thence the love of education has been disseminated over all the northern and western portions of the Union. The State of New York, moved, I believe, by the venerable man, whose efforts in the cause of education we have met to celebrate, at an early period established a magnificent fund for the support of public schools. It is cheering to observe the rapidity with which this spirit has been diffused throughout the Western States. I believe that the man is still living who erected the first cabin on the spot now known as the city of Cincinnati. At the present moment, the provisions of Ohio for common school education are inferior to none in our country, and the schools of the Queen City of the West do not decline a comparison with those of any city in the land.

The influence of these examples has pervaded the general government itself. Hence, in the organization of the new States, if I do not misremember, provision is always made for public education, by reserving large tracts of land to be forever appropriated to this purpose. A permanent foundation is thus laid for the universal education of the people. Some of this land has been appropriated to university education, and hence a provision is made for the establishment of seats of learning, in what was very lately a wilderness, which will vie in extent and magnificence with those in any part of the world.

The result of all this may be easily imagined. A common school education, good now, and every year growing better, is placed within the reach of every child in the older Free States, and in the new States where it is not rendered impracticable by sparseness of population; and of these advantages the people very generally avail themselves. Reading and writing, and the ordinary branches of school education, are the acquisition of every child. Even among our English ancestors, formerly, I might almost say now, these were rare accomplishments which conferred on their possessor an enviable distinction. Among us, they have long since ceased to be a distinction, while to be unable to read or write is an acknowledged disgrace. When a man cannot sign his name, it is taken for granted that he is not a native-born American.

The result of all this has been that, at the present moment, there are probably more readers of the English language in the United States than in all the world beside. Instead of being merely a province, we are becoming the chief seat of the Anglo-Saxon nation. If I remember correctly, Macaulay's History of England had not been published six months, before ten times as many copies had been printed in this country as in England. Long before this time, I presume that this disproportion has been doubled. It has been printed in every variety of form, as cheap as twenty-five cents a volume, thus showing that its circulation penetrated every rank of society. The same fact is illustrated by the vast number of newspapers published in this country. Every man reads them, and every man whom you meet is acquainted with the news of the day. The increasing amount of authorship is an indication of the same character. A large proportion of this authorship, moreover, proceeds from persons who have received no aid from collegiate education. The remark of HORACE is specially true of us; *docti et indocti*— he might have said, *indoctæ — scribimus.* A large number of our most acceptable writers are women, who are excluded from our colleges. A very respectable periodical was for some time, I know not but it is still, conducted by the factory girls at Lowell. Such facts as these indicate the extent and the excellence of the education which is offered freely to every young person among us. The intellectual culture of Americans who labor has been frequently remarked by intelligent foreigners. To this they have ascribed our unparalleled progress in the arts. The best English writers on this subject, at the present day, urge this as a reason why education, and good education, should be universally diffused among the working classes at home. They acknowledge us to be their rivals in all the useful arts, and they confess that they must be distanced in the race, unless they can elevate the standard of intellectual attainment in their people, to a level with our own.

When we speak of higher, or, as it is called, collegiate education, we mean that course of instruction which begins when common or school education ends. Now I ask, in view of these facts, when did a people exist that ever presented such a field for this kind of instruction? When the whole mass of mind is thus quickened, remarkable talents, those endowments which God has bestowed for the good of the whole, cannot but display themselves. What we seem specially to need, is the means of developing such talent in every direction, so that not one of these special gifts of God may be lost. Distinguished talent for any thing, is one of the most signal blessings ever bestowed upon man, and we are false to ourselves, and ungrateful to our Creator, if we do not improve it all, and improve it to the uttermost.

I will mention only one other peculiarity of the condition of this country: it is that our institutions are in every respect thoroughly democratic.

Democracy supposes that the object of society is simple, that it is to confirm every man in the enjoyment of all the means of happiness bestowed upon him by his Creator. It takes it for granted that *every man has a right to himself*, and to all the innocent results of the use of his faculties. The object of society, and of government, which is its agent, is to guarantee to every individual the full possession of this right. This obligation, in the formation of a civil polity, men mutually assume toward each other. This, then, is the essential limit of the power of society over the individual. If, for mutual convenience, any other power is entrusted to society, it is always done on the condition that it be exercised for the good of every member equally, for all the members being equal, no power can be rightly exerted for the benefit of the one, unless it be also exercised for the benefit of all.

Beyond this, democratic society does not interfere. It leaves the individual to work out his own destiny for himself. Every man is thus made the architect of his own fortune. If he succeed, he alone is entitled to the advantages of his success. If he fail, it is the result of his own voluntary action, for which he has no one to blame but himself. Every individual is allowed to pursue his own happiness, in his own way, and all that society does is to protect him from the interference of his neighbor. If it ever attempts to confer any aid, it confers it equally upon all, knowing no distinction between the high or low, the rich or poor; but looking upon them all from one single point of view, that is, as members of society.

The responsibility of every individual's success or failure, is thus thrown wholly upon himself. Hence arises the intense activity which pervades republican institutions. Every motive power has free and unembarrassed action. Universal competition gives intensity to every effort. Every inducement is spread before every individual to benefit his condition by every means in his power. The spirit pervades the whole social mass. Every atom becomes vital. Every man has a distinct object to be accomplished, and he knows that it can be accomplished only by putting forth all the power with which he has been endowed. To this we owe that self-reliance and adaptation to every condition which is said to distinguish our countrymen. Go where you will, from the equator to the pole, you will every where find the representatives of the "Universal Yankee Nation," and you will generally find them intelligent, enterprising, laborious, and therefore successful.

Now, it can scarcely have escaped the notice of such a people, that the practice of every art depends for success on a knowledge of some social or physical law. Knowledge, to every intelligent man, is emphatically power. If he fail in any art, he knows that it must have been because he has violated some law; if he succeed, it must be because he has obeyed it. To such a community, knowledge is then a matter of imperative necessity. This is the very element of success. Without it, unless by accident, man must labor in vain, and consume his capital without remuneration. Hence, it may readily be believed that such a people would eagerly desire that physical knowledge, on which all success in the useful arts depends, as well as that other spiritual knowledge which the human mind instinctively craves, as soon as its energies are aroused, and the true and the beautiful are brought within its field of vision.

That such is becoming rapidly the tendency of this country, must, I think, be evident. It is obvious from the wonderful development of the talent for invention, for which we are remarkable. It is shown in the earnest endeavor to improve our school system, to which I have already alluded. It is proved by the immense sums, bestowed in every part of our land, for the endowment of institutions of learning; a very large part of which is given by men who have acquired their wealth by the labor of their hands. If it be said that, after all, the men who avail themselves of the laws of nature in their daily pursuits, do not resort to our colleges, the reply is easy. We may well ask, if they resorted thither would they find what they wanted? Our teaching of nature's laws is designed not for men who expect to use their knowledge, but for those who expect immediately to forget it. Let, however, instruction be given, adapted to the wants of the community, on any scientific subject, and the instructor, wherever he can find men, will rarely want for hearers.

Such, then, is the condition of our people. We have a population increasing in wealth with a rapidity wholly unprecedented. The intellect of this people is aroused to action by the means universally provided for common school education. This awakened intellect is stimulated to uncommon activity by the legitimate effects of the democratic principle. Now, can a philanthropist, a patriot, or a statesman, hesitate for a moment, when he is called upon to determine the principles by which the higher education of such a people should be governed?

Shall we, having educated the whole people up to a certain point, giving to all equal advantages for self-development, then reverse our whole system, and bestow the advantages of higher education only upon a few? Shall we say that the lawyer, and physician, and clergyman, need a knowledge of principles in order to pursue their callings with success, while the farmer, the mechanic, the manufacturer, and the merchant require no knowledge of the laws upon which the success of every operation which they perform depends? Shall we say that we need a literary class of men, and for the education of these we will make ample provision, while for all the rest it makes no manner of difference whether they be thoughtful, independent and self-reliant, or nothing but mere hewers of wood and drawers of water? Shall we say that intellect is to be cultivated and talent developed in one direction alone, or developed in every possible direction? I cannot conceive it possible for American citizens to hold any divided opinion on this subject. He would certainly be a rare man who would openly contend for such a distinction as these questions suppose. We are all equal. We are all left each one for himself to work out his own destiny, and to make provision for those that shall come after him. Every one needs knowledge, knowledge of the laws which shall command success in his own avocation. Every one needs that knowledge which shall enable him to form correct judgments, and all men need it equally. Wherever a provision is made for education by private munificence, all men may reasonably expect to share it without distinction; where provision is made by the public, they may rightfully demand it. Nothing can be conceived of, more diametrically opposed to the first principles of our government, than to impose a tax upon the whole, and then appropriate it to the benefit of a part.

But it will, I presume, be answered, that I am contending where there is no adversary; that all our institutions of learning are equally open for all, and that all men may avail themselves of their advantages if they be so disposed. All this I grant. But I ask, for whom were our present systems of collegiate education devised? — for the few or for the many? They were originally designed exclusively for the clergy, and in the fatherland they have been perpetuated for the clergy and the aristocracy. They are, in this country, devised mainly for the professions, and their success is measured by their results upon the professions. The learning which they cultivate is in kind and amount measured by the demands of the professions. But I ask, as I have done before, have not the mechanic and the merchant, the farmer and the manufacturer, as much need of knowledge, each in his own profession, as the lawyer, the minister, and the physician? Have they not as just a claim on the money taken from their own earnings, as those classes which have been so exclusively favored? May they not then justly demand that not only education in higher knowledge shall be provided for them, but that it shall be education of which they may profitably avail themselves; so that they may enter upon their career in life, under as favorable auspices as those who prefer what are sometimes called literary professions?

It would seem then that, in devising a system of higher education for our country, we should commence with the self-evident maxim, that we are to labor not for the benefit of one but of all; not for a caste, or a clique, but for the whole community. Proceeding upon this ground, we should provide the instruction needed by every class of our fellow-citizens. Wherever an institution is established in any part of our country, our first inquiry should be, what is the kind of knowledge (in addition to that demanded for all) which this portion of our people needs, in order to perfect them in their professions, give them power over principles, enable them to develop their intellectual resources and employ their talents to the greatest advantage for themselves and for the country? This knowledge, whatever it may be, should be provided as liberally for one class as for another. Whatever is thus taught, however, should be taught, not only with the design of increasing knowledge, but also of giving strength, enlargement and skill to the original faculties of the soul. When a system of education formed on these principles shall pervade this country, we may be able to present to the world the legitimate results of free institutions; by pursuing any other career we may render them a shame and a by-word.

Who can fail to see that the universal dissemination of the most valuable knowledge is imperatively demanded by the present condition of our country. We possess a territory of boundless extent, embracing every variety of soil. This immense domain can never be taught to yield its richest and most abundant products, until the knowledge of vegetable and animal physiology, the chemical constituents of soils, meteorology, and physical geography shall have been made the common property of all our citizens. The mineral wealth of all this region is yet unknown, except in those localities where it has obtruded itself upon the surface. Scientific mining and geology can alone reveal to us the treasures which lie beneath the soil, warning us against absurd explorations, and pointing out to us the spots where our labors will be rewarded with abundant success. To accomplish this result, however, it will not be sufficient to teach merely such an amount of physical science as may be required by a lawyer or a clergyman; but these departments must be elevated into thorough courses of study, designed for and adapted to the wants of those who need their aid in advancing the material progress of our country.

But, after all, the most valuable treasures which God bestows upon every country is found in the spiritual nature of man. Distinguished talent, if it be only guided by virtue, is the richest gift which is ever lavished upon a nation. Native talent is probably given in larger measure to those who labor (provided their labor is not exhausting and brutalizing) than to other men. Hence it is, that, in revolutions when great ability is required, it is generally found to exist in the middle classes. Physical labor cultivates mental energy, resolution, and self-reliance; all prime elements in the formation of eminent character. It is from this range of condition that invention generally proceeds, that wonderful talent which, within the last century, has wrought so mighty changes in the aspects of civilization. From the minds of WATT, ARKWRIGHT, and STEPHENSON, have originated those combinations that have opened so glorious a path for the progress of humanity. In our own country, the wonderful increase of the cotton culture, and the incidental and fearful growth of the slave power, is all to be ascribed to the cotton-gin of ELI WHITNEY. It is to the genius of FULTON that we owe the development of the mighty west; and the transfer of the dominion of this country from the eastern to the western slope of the Alleghanies. We have now the most intelligent and self-reliant mechanics on earth. We need nothing more than to spread a knowledge of the laws of nature among those who daily, without knowing how, put them in practice, to give this country unapproachable precedence in the useful arts. The results of this universal diffusion of knowledge, upon science, literature and discovery, are obvious; but my limits do not allow me to treat of them in detail.

The present is a most auspicious moment in which to take this subject into full consideration. There seems a fatal tendency, in the formation of systems of education, blindly to follow precedents, without examining the laws on which they are founded, or the results which they have attained. The west, in organizing its institutions, looks backward to the east, and considers its labor perfected when it has copied the universal model. We of the east, as far as public opinion will permit, have imitated Cambridge and Oxford, without considering how utterly unsuited to our condition must be institutions founded for the education of the mediœval clergy, and modified by the pressure of an all-powerful aristocracy. But the spirit of reform, originating from without, is already transforming these venerable seats of learning. It is confessed that they are wholly unadapted to meet the wants of the Great Britain of the present, and the nation insists that their character must be changed. They must be open to all, and they must teach the knowledge which England needs. Such are the demands of humanity, and these demands must be satisfied. Is it not becoming in us to follow this example? Is it not imperative on us to set an example for ourselves? In a free country like our own, unembarrassed by precedents, and not yet entangled by the vested rights of by-gone ages, ought we not to originate a system of education which shall raise to high intellectual culture the whole mass of our people? When our systems of education shall look with as kindly an eye on the mechanic as the lawyer, on the manufacturer and merchant as the minister; when every artizan, performing his process with a knowledge of the laws by which it is governed, shall be transformed from an unthinking laborer into a practical philosopher; and when the benign principles of Christianity shall imbue the whole mass of our people with the spirit of universal love, then, and not till then, shall we illustrate to the nations the blessings of Republican and Christian Institutions.

You all perceive that the line of remark which I have here pursued, has been suggested by the circumstances of the present memorable occasion. An aged man, the Nestor of American teachers, finds himself this day surrounded by pupils who have assembled from every State in our Union, to offer him their filial congratulations. An officer of instruction, who has for half a century presided over a most flourishing seat of learning, is here met by the thousands who have returned to the home of their education, to declare that whatever of success they have achieved in their several professions, has been greatly owing to the wisdom of his precepts and the purity of his example. He who, while discharging with unrivalled

ability the duties of the lecture room, and watching with parental solicitude over the individual development of every pupil committed to his charge, has yet found time, by masterly skill, to accumulate a fund which must render Union College the most favored institution in our country, has this year completed his labor, and has laid this magnificent offering on the altar of public education. While for fifty years distributing gratuitous instruction with profuse liberality, he has been also providing the means for a wider and richer distribution of its blessings for all coming time. A benignant Providence has spared that honored life, and crowned those labors with triumphant success; and now a whole community, uttering the voice of humanity, has assembled to bow in grateful reverence before that hoary head, which, for half a century, has been encircled with the wreath of profound learning, matchless sagacity, unwearied benevolence, surpassing eloquence, and childlike piety. The youth and the age of the present seem here to unite with the coming generations of the future, and shower on the head of that "old man eloquent" their selectest benedictions.

Venerable man! We rejoice to see that thine eye is not dim, though thy natural force is somewhat abated. We thank you for your care over our youth; we thank you for those counsels which have so often guided our manhood; we thank you for that example which has ever so clearly pointed out to us the path of earnest duty and self-forgetful charity. Long may you yet live to witness the happiness which you have created, and cherish the genius which your inspirations first awakened to conscious existence. And when the Saviour, in whose footsteps you have trodden, shall call thee home to receive thy reward, may death lay his hand gently on that venerated form, and gently quiet the pulsations of that noble heart. May thy fainting head recline upon the bosom of the Redeemer whom thou hast loved; may thine eye open upon visions of glory which man may not utter; and so may an entrance be abundantly administered to thee into the joy of thy Lord. Heaven will account itself richer, as it opens its pearly gates to welcome thy approach; but where shall those who survive find any thing left on earth that resembles thee?

www.ingramcontent.com/pod-product-compliance
Lightning Source LLC
LaVergne TN
LVHW011133110826
845150LV00008B/2329

* 9 7 8 1 4 1 8 1 9 4 2 8 4 *